Yasser ARAFAT

KT-512-592

DAVID DOWNING

Heinemann LIBRARY

H www.heinemann.co.uk

Visit our website to find out more information about Heinemann Library books.

To order:

☎ Phone 44 (0) 1865 888066

▤ Send a fax to 44 (0) 1865 314091

▥ Visit the Heinemann Bookshop at www.heinemann.co.uk to browse our catalogue and order online.

First published in Great Britain by Heinemann Library,
Halley Court, Jordan Hill, Oxford OX2 8EJ,
a division of Reed Educational and Professional Publishing Ltd.
Heinemann is a registered trademark of Reed Educational and Professional Publishing Ltd.

OXFORD MELBOURNE AUCKLAND
JOHANNESBURG BLANTYRE GABORONE
IBADAN PORTSMOUTH (NH) USA CHICAGO

© Reed Educational and Professional Publishing Ltd 2002
The moral right of the proprietor has been asserted.

Designed by AMR
Illustrated by Art Construction
Originated by Dot Gradations
Printed in China

ISBN 0 431 13865 6 (hardback)
06 05 04 03
10 9 8 7 6 5 4 3 2

ISBN 0 431 13872 9 (paperback)
07 06 05 04 03
10 9 8 7 6 5 4 3 2 1

British Library Cataloguing in Publication Data
Downing, David
  Yasser Arafat. – (Leading lives)
  1.Arafat, Yasir 2.Heads of state – Palestine – Biography – Juvenile literature
  3.Palestine – Politics and government – 1948– – Juvenile literature
  4.Palestine – History – Juvenile literature
  I.Title
  322.4'2'092

Acknowledgements
The publishers would like to thank the following for permission to reproduce photographs: Associated Press: pp. 40, 53, 55; Camera Press: p. 42; Camera Press/John Tordai: p. 39; Corbis: pp. 10, 16, 17, 26, 34; G. Chauvel/Sygma: pp. 21, 23; Hulton Archive: pp. 29, 47; Popperfoto: pp. 9, 11, 15, 18, 37, 43, 48, 49, 51; Topham: pp. 5, 24, 31, 33, 45.

Cover photograph reproduced with permission of Camera Press.

Every effort has been made to contact copyright holders of any material reproduced in this book. Any omissions will be rectified in subsequent printings if notice is given to the publishers.

Our thanks to Christopher Gibb for his comments in the preparation of this book.

Disclaimer
All the Internet addresses (URLs) given in this book were valid at the time of going to press. However, due to the dynamic nature of the Internet, some addresses may have changed, or sites may have ceased to exist since publication. While the author and publishers regret any inconvenience this may cause readers, no responsibility for any such changes can be accepted by either the author or the publishers.

Any words appearing in the text in bold, **like this**, are explained in the Glossary.

Contents

Into the spotlight

It is almost dawn in the valley of the River Jordan, on 21 March 1968. Three columns of Israeli tanks rumble across bridges, heading for the Jordanian village of Karameh, some 6 kilometres (4 miles) to the east. Here Yasser Arafat, the leader of the Palestinian **guerrilla fighters**, has set up his headquarters.

The Israelis are confident of victory. They know there are only some 300 **Palestinian** fighters in Karameh, and they are not worried by the presence nearby of Jordanian army units. Only nine months have passed since they defeated the **Arab** armies of three states in less than a week. By nightfall, they expect to have killed or captured most of the Palestinians, including their leader.

In Karameh, Arafat and his men – some old, some merely children – are waiting for the attack. Some of his colleagues have argued in favour of retreat, but Arafat has refused. As a student leader in Egypt, as a *fedayeen* raider into Israel, as the inspiration behind the guerrilla group named **Fatah**, which he now leads, he has always been both stubborn and brave. 'We cannot defeat them,' he tells his men, 'but we can teach them a lesson.'

The sky is lightening as the Israelis reach Karameh. Low cloud limits the amount of air support their ground troops can expect, but the Israelis' only real worry is that they have arrived too late: the village seems deserted. Then suddenly Arafat's troops are among them, leaping aboard the tanks and dropping grenades inside them.

The Israelis recover from the shock and continue their attacks, but the Palestinians fight on, house by house and

▲ *Israeli troops enter the Jordanian village of Karameh on 21 March 1968. Arafat became an overnight hero for his leadership of the Palestinian resistance to this attack.*

street by street. By midday a third of Arafat's fighters are dead, and defeat seems certain. They are saved by the Jordanians, who have been watching the battle from the hills to the east, and who now open fire on the surprised Israelis. Arafat and his men take their chance to re-group, and the Israelis decide that enough is enough. They pull their forces back across the River Jordan.

Unfairly, but understandably, Arafat and Fatah claim all the credit for victory. Until this moment the 38-year-old leader has been virtually unknown outside Palestinian circles, but now photographs of his pudgy, unshaven face and trademark traditional cloth head-dress are everywhere. Arafat's defiance has brought himself and his people into the world spotlight, and he will spend the rest of his life making sure that they stay there. For the next 30 years he and the cause of his people will become impossible to separate.

Childhood and youth

On 24 August 1929, Zahwa Abul Saoud, the wife of Abdel Raouf Arafat Al Qudua Al Husseini, gave birth to their sixth child. They named him Mohammed Abdel Rahman Abdel Raouf Arafat Al Qudua Al Husseini, but the world would later come to know him as Yasser (or Yasir) Arafat. He was called Yasser – which means 'easy-going' – from a very early age. However, the eventual decision to link it with Arafat – his paternal grandfather's name – was his alone.

His place of birth remains in doubt. Arafat has often told journalists that he was born in Jerusalem, then the administrative centre of the British-ruled territory of Palestine. However, it seems more likely that he was born in Cairo, the capital of neighbouring Egypt. By the 1920s Egypt had its own king and parliament, but its real rulers remained the British.

There is no doubt that Yasser's parents moved to Cairo in 1927, but why they left their home in the **Palestinian** town of Gaza remains something of a mystery. Some historians claim that Abdel Raouf, a reasonably prosperous merchant, had angered local people by trading with Jewish immigrants; others that he was eager to claim land and property in Cairo that he thought belonged to his family. He certainly spent much of the next 20 years trying to prove that claim.

Boyhood in Jerusalem and Cairo

In 1933, Yasser's mother Zahwa died suddenly of a kidney illness. His elder brothers and sisters – Inam, Khalid, Yusar, Mustapha and Khadija – stayed in Cairo, but Yasser and his younger brother Fathi were sent to live with their mother's family, the Abul Saouds, in their compound adjoining the famous **Western Wall** in Jerusalem. The Abul Saouds were not rich, but their home was welcoming, and Yasser would always remember his time in Jerusalem with great affection.

Palestine

The name Palestine is usually applied to that area of land at the eastern end of the Mediterranean sea which the British ruled between 1918 and 1948. In ancient times this area was inhabited by many different peoples, and came to be known as the Holy Land because of its importance to the **Jewish**, **Christian** and **Muslim** religions. From around AD 700 to 1918 it was almost continuously ruled and mostly inhabited by Muslims.

From the late 19th century onwards, there was significant Jewish **emigration** to Palestine. This emigration was encouraged by the British decision, spelt out in the **Balfour Declaration** of 1917, to look favourably on the creation of a Jewish homeland in the territory, and accelerated by the increasing **persecution** of European Jews, which climaxed in the horrors of the **Holocaust**, in which six million Jews were murdered.

However, the British had also promised the Muslim **Arab** population of Palestine that nothing would be done 'to prejudice the civil and religious rights of existing non-Jewish communities', and most Arabs resented the increase in Jewish **immigration**. By effectively promising Palestine to both peoples, the British made a fight for control of the territory almost inevitable.

Yasser's early life in Jerusalem also introduced him to politics. Palestine's Arab majority was angry at the British for allowing so much Jewish immigration, and the years 1936–39 were marked by strikes, demonstrations and widespread violence. Like many other Arab children, the seven-year-old Yasser put nails on the road, slashed tyres and threw stones at the British. According to some reports he was slapped by one of the British officers who came to question his uncle, Selim Abul Saoud.

For several years Yasser and Fathi were shuttled back and forth between Cairo and Jerusalem, but when Yasser was eight (some historians say thirteen) the two boys were finally sent back to Cairo. The family lived in a seven-room apartment in the prosperous district of Abbasiya, and there is no reason to believe they ever experienced any real hardship. But the atmosphere was less loving than it had been in Jerusalem, mostly because the children were unable to get on with either their father's second wife or his third wife. Abdel Raouf grew increasingly obsessed by his legal claim, and left the care of the younger children to his eldest daughter Inam, who was now in her late teens.

Very little is known about Yasser as a boy. According to Inam he liked making army camps in the garden of their house, which he filled with other local boys. Brother Fathi remembered Yasser putting metal dish 'helmets' on his followers' heads and marching them up and down the street, striking them with a stick if they disobeyed.

He had charm, and he was always generous. 'Yasser shared everything with everybody,' Inam said. 'Even the smallest piece of chocolate was shared with others. He never cared about himself.' Both the desire to lead and the lack of interest in possessions would stay with him throughout his life.

The young boy

'What little is known about young Yasser during this period suggests a hyperactive, intelligent child who, despite being undisciplined, was capable of easy achievement and of endearing himself to the people around him ...'

(Biographer Said K. Aburish, describing Arafat during his boyhood years in Jerusalem)

Teenage politics

In his teens Yasser developed an interest in politics, and his sister often found him and his friends deep in political discussion when they were supposed to be doing their homework. He attended many of the demonstrations that took place against the British during this time. World War II was now under way, and the British were no longer bothering to hide the fact that they, and not the Egyptians, were the real rulers of Egypt.

▲ *The Western or 'Wailing' Wall in Jerusalem. Arafat lived in a compound adjoining the wall when he was a child.*

▲ *The city which Arafat knew as a teenager: the Egyptian capital Cairo in 1942.*

In 1945 the war ended, and the following year two important visitors arrived in Cairo. One was the **Mufti** of Jerusalem, Hajj Amin Al Husseini, who had led the Palestine rebellion against the British in 1936. The other was the Mufti's assistant, Sheikh Hassan Abul Saoud, head of Yasser's mother's family with whom Yasser had once lived in Jerusalem.

The seventeen-year-old Yasser became Sheikh Hassan's unofficial assistant. He sharpened pencils, supplied glasses of cold water, delivered letters and collected money for the Palestinian cause. He began to learn what politics were all about.

Student

As a boy, Yasser had always shown an interest in mechanical things and how they worked, so no one in his family was very surprised when he chose to study engineering at King Fuad I (later Cairo) University. The **Mufti** and Sheikh Hassan may have helped him with his fees; Yasser's father was too involved in his legal battle for family land to take much interest in his son's education. He finally lost his case in 1948, and died four years later. Yasser chose not to attend the funeral.

The birth of a fighter

At college Yasser neither studied hard nor behaved like a typical student. He neither drank nor smoked, and seemed completely uninterested in women. All he cared about were politics, which were 'the dream and hope of his life', according to one college friend.

◀ King Fuad I of Egypt in 1913, at about the time the university named after him was being constructed. Yasser attended the university from 1949 to 1956.

Angry young man

'He was a strange young man. He had a certain charm which he could use to great advantage. But he also had a dark streak, a sort of permanent irrational anger that was simmering below the surface.'

(Jinan Al-Oraby, who knew Arafat in the 1950s)

As a **Palestinian** who had spent most of his life in Egypt, the young Arafat was interested in both Palestinian and Egyptian politics. The main issues in the two countries were different – modernization (bringing up to date with the latest ideas and technology) in Egypt and **immigration** by **Jews** in Palestine – but there were also important similarities. In both countries **Arabs** were trying to get rid of those they considered foreign intruders – the Jews and British in Palestine, the British in Egypt. He also helped to organize military training for himself and other Palestinian students at the university, and on one occasion showed an early glimpse of his flair for **public relations**, buying up a battered armoured car from a scrap metal dealer and dramatically placing it at the centre of a big public demonstration against the planned partition of Palestine (see box on page 14).

War broke out in Palestine in late 1947 when the British, exhausted by World War II and tired of being shot at by both sides, left. Arafat and other students rushed off to join the fighting. After crossing the Suez Canal in a small boat in the dead of night, Arafat eventually joined an Egyptian **Muslim Brotherhood** unit in the Gaza area. He later exaggerated his exploits, claiming to have destroyed one column of tanks almost single-handedly, but the truth was impressive enough. His bravery under fire, on this and many future occasions, would be one of the major reasons for his popularity.

The war lost, he returned to Cairo. Unlike thousands of his fellow Palestinians, he had not been driven from his home to a faraway **refugee camp**, but he still felt the humiliation and loss. He blamed the Israelis for, as he saw it, stealing his people's land, and the other Arab states for letting them get away with it.

Student leader

Arafat involved himself with student politics, continued with his military training classes, and took time off to join Muslim Brotherhood raids against the British authorities in the **Suez Canal Zone**. In 1952, he stood for the presidency of the Palestinian Student Federation (PSF), and demonstrated the ability to make people think he was on their side that would be so useful in his future career. When he was with Muslim Brotherhood sympathizers he talked like a Muslim, when he was with **Communists** he talked like a Communist, and so on. In reality, he was a Palestinian **nationalist** and little else. He had little interest in those issues that divide most politicians, issues which deal with how a society is organized. He was only interested in there actually being a Palestinian society, and in his role in creating one.

Around this time he met one of the two men who would become his closest political companions. Abu Iyad played a large part in getting Arafat elected to the PSF presidency, and between them they launched a newspaper called *The Voice of Palestine*, which helped keep alive the idea of a Palestinian identity.

FOR DETAILS ON KEY PEOPLE OF ARAFAT'S TIME, SEE PAGES 59–60.

The partition of Palestine and the war of 1947–49

After World War II and the **Holocaust** the number of Jews **emigrating** to Palestine rose dramatically. In 1947 the British, unable to control the growing conflict between Arabs and Jews, handed the problem over to the **United Nations** (**UN**). A plan to divide or 'partition' Palestine into Jewish and Arab states was announced on 29 November 1947. The Palestinian Arabs refused to accept any sort of **partition**, and full **civil war** broke out between them and the Jews. The better-organized Jews soon gained the upper hand, and in May 1948 they proclaimed the state of Israel in those areas of Palestine which they now controlled.

Five Arab states – Egypt, Lebanon, Syria, Transjordan and Iraq – sent armies in to destroy this new state, but were all defeated. By early 1949 an Israel considerably larger than that proposed in the UN partition plan was firmly established, and the remaining Arab-controlled areas of Palestine – the so-called **Gaza Strip** and a much larger area west of the Jordan river (later known as the **West Bank**) – were swallowed up by Egypt and Transjordan (later Jordan) respectively. Palestine, as an Arab area in its own right, had been wiped from the map.

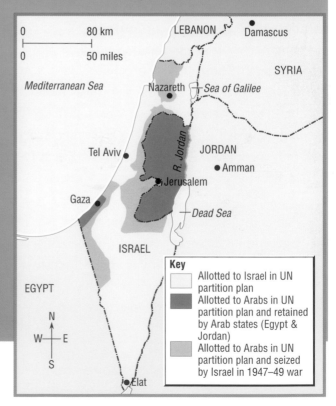

0   80 km
0   50 miles

Mediterranean Sea

LEBANON   • Damascus

SYRIA

Nazareth   Sea of Galilee

R. Jordan

Tel Aviv •

JORDAN

• Amman

• Jerusalem

Gaza •

Dead Sea

ISRAEL

EGYPT

N
W—E
S

• Élat

Key

☐ Allotted to Israel in UN partition plan

■ Allotted to Arabs in UN partition plan and retained by Arab states (Egypt & Jordan)

▨ Allotted to Arabs in UN partition plan and seized by Israel in 1947–49 war

The Suez War

In 1952, the Egyptian government was overthrown by a group
of army officers (the Free Officers' Movement, led by Gamal
Abdel Nasser). General Neguib became President, but it was
his right-hand man, Colonel Nasser, who really took control.
Nasser was an Arab nationalist, and at first he encouraged the
Palestinian fighters or *fedayeen* to launch raids against Israel
from the Egyptian-occupied **Gaza Strip**. Arafat, still
supposedly a student, took part in several of these raids. One
of the *fedayeen* leaders he met during this period was Abu
Jihad, who would become his second great political ally.

▲ *British planes patrol the Suez Canal, partly in response to the hit-and-run
raids of Egyptian nationalists.*

In 1956 Arafat and Abu Iyad attended a student conference in Prague, then the capital of communist Czechoslovakia. To his friends' surprise Arafat turned up at one session wearing a traditional Arab head-dress or *kuffiya*, which in the 1930s had become a symbol of Palestinian resistance. By wearing one Arafat both advertised the cause and made himself stand out. It was another example of his flair for public relations.

While Arafat was in Prague, President Nasser **nationalized** the Suez Canal, which further deepened the existing hostility between the Western powers, Britain and France, and Egypt. That autumn Britain and France tried to take the canal back by force, and as part of their plan they invited the Israelis to occupy Egypt's Sinai Peninsula. The Anglo-French occupation proved a disaster, but the Israeli attack was a spectacular success, and the Israeli Government refused to give up Sinai until the UN deployed soldiers along the Israeli–Egyptian border. The presence of these soldiers meant an end to *fedayeen* raids across that border.

▲ Soon after announcing that he has taken over the Suez Canal, Egypt's President Nasser is cheered by a huge crowd in Cairo, August 1956.

The newly graduated Arafat, now 27 years old, had considered joining the *fedayeen* on a full-time basis, but now he had to think again. What was he to do with the rest of his life? He was determined to fight on against the Israeli occupation of his homeland, but he also had to earn a living.

Fatah

Like many other **Palestinians** at this time, Arafat decided to move to one of the newly oil-rich states of the Persian Gulf. His first choice was Saudi Arabia, but his work permit was slow in arriving, and he accepted the offer of an engineering job with the Ministry of Public Works in the Gulf kingdom of Kuwait. His salary for supervising the construction of roads and bridges was around $30,000 a year, a substantial sum in 1957.

▶ Oil pipelines snaking towards the sea in Kuwait City, where Arafat and other Palestinians went to work.

The founding of Fatah

Over the next couple of years many of Arafat's colleagues from his student and *fedayeen* days also arrived in Kuwait. Abu Jihad and Abu Iyad both took teaching jobs; others worked, like Arafat, in industry. This group of young Palestinians all needed to work, but they also wanted that sense of companionship which their shared experience as politically motivated Palestinians gave them. They spent many long nights discussing their plans for freeing their homeland.

In 1959, the group took several important steps. They formed an organization that they named **Fatah** – 'conquest' in Arabic – and launched a magazine called *Our Palestine, The Call of Life* to publicize its ideas. Fatah's main aim was the destruction of Israel, and they hoped to achieve this through a purely Palestinian armed struggle. They expected no real help from the **Arab** states, and had no desire to tie themselves to a particular sponsor.

They also refused to commit themselves to any political ideology: Fatah was neither Conservative nor Socialist nor **Communist** – it was a **nationalist** movement. Like Arafat the student leader, Fatah wanted to appeal to all Palestinians, regardless of their political beliefs.

▲ *A Palestinian refugee camp in northern Jordan. Most of the occupants had lost their homes when the old territory of Palestine came under Israeli control.*

Snapshot of a bachelor

As word of Fatah slowly spread through the Palestinian **diaspora**, Arafat continued with his engineering work. He lived alone in a bungalow and spent most of his money on clothes and cars. Friends remember him fashionably dressed in a shiny white sports coat and black sharkskin trousers, and he sometimes drove his favourite two-tone Thunderbird convertible across the desert to shop in the boutiques of Baghdad or Beirut. 'The only fault with Arafat's driving,' one friend said, was that 'all the time he is driving he talks and uses his hands.'

At home he loved watching cartoons on television – *Road Runner* and *Tom and Jerry* were his particular favourites. All he ever read were newspapers, which provided him with the information he needed for the political arguments that filled so many evenings. Often these finished so late that he ended up sleeping on a friend's couch or floor.

Paying for someone else's crime

'We Arabs did not kill six million Jews or persecute them. Europeans did that. But we Arabs paid the price. I think I'm entitled to say that life has not been very fair to us.'

(Yasser Arafat, talking about the **Holocaust** in Europe)

The armed struggle

Through the early 1960s the preparations for Fatah's armed struggle went on. Money was raised from wealthy Palestinians working in the Gulf area and the royal families of several Arab states. Fighters were recruited and training camps set up in Algeria, Lebanon and Syria. In 1963, Arafat finally gave up his job in Kuwait, moved to Syria, and devoted himself full time to Fatah. He had made enough money to last him for several years.

'Dog's sense'

According to Arafat, his closest call was in a small village. 'This was my headquarters,' he says. 'At eleven I got up. I don't know why. There were only two of us in the house and I said, "we should leave"....'

When his associate asked him why, Arafat told him, 'I feel we are in danger.' The friend argued and went outside to look around, insisting there was no danger. Arafat grew angry and said, 'We have to leave. If not I will leave alone.'

The two men walked to the village of Deir Salam and arrived there just towards dawn. 'We looked back to see where we had left,' says Arafat, 'and there were army vehicles. When he turned around, my friend began to weep with joy.'

Arafat calls this intuition his 'dog's sense'.

(From John and Janet Wallach's *Arafat in the Eyes of the Beholder*)

In 1964, the first Fatah organizers were sent into the area of Jordan (the **West Bank**) which offered the easiest access to Israel. Their job was to make contacts and prepare the ground for the later **infiltration** of fighters. The first real raid took place in January 1965. Several men sneaked across the border into Israel and left sticks of dynamite in a canal. They were discovered before they exploded.

This was an unfortunate start, and things hardly improved as the year progressed. Raid followed raid, but, in the beginning at least, the Israeli authorities were more irritated than alarmed. Arafat was the only one of the Fatah leaders actually to go on these raids, and in the process he began to demonstrate the two aspects of his character that would colour his whole career.

The first of these aspects was his reluctance to take directions from anyone else. He organized and conducted raids and spent Fatah's money as he saw fit. In May 1966 he was actually suspended by his colleagues for his refusal to respect the principle of collective (shared) leadership.

But the second of these aspects made him irreplaceable, and the suspension was soon lifted. Put simply, Arafat was an inspiration to those around him. He was brave, imaginative and utterly determined. His love of disguises – in these raids he made appearances as an Egyptian tourist, a Pakistani businessman, a shepherd and a lost old man – was the stuff of legend. He was the ideal role model for Fatah's recruits.

The raids were not doing much damage to the Israelis, but for the moment that did not matter. The important thing was that Arafat and Fatah were refusing to accept defeat or let the Palestinian cause fade from sight. By showing that something could be done, they shamed the other Arab leaders into mounting their own attacks on Israel, at first with words, and then with the aggressive actions that provoked the Six Day War of June 1967.

▶ *Arafat in Jordan. He enjoyed being able to look like different characters so that he could cross the border into Israel and plan raids for the Fatah organization.*

Guerrilla hero

In June 1967 Israel, expecting an attack from its **Arab** neighbours, struck the first blow of what was called the Six Day War or the June War. The Arab air forces were destroyed on the ground, and within six days Arab armies had been completely defeated. Egyptian Sinai and the **Gaza Strip**, the Jordanian **West Bank** and East Jerusalem, and the Syrian Golan Heights all passed into Israeli occupation. The old territory of Palestine was now completely under Israeli control. The leaders of the Arab states, their armies humiliated by Israeli forces a fraction of their size, lost all their credibility.

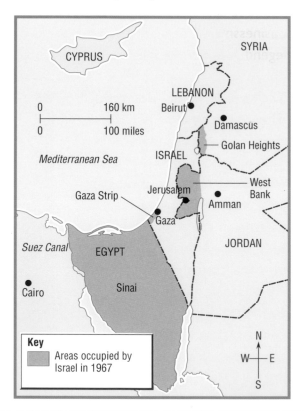

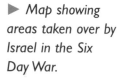 ► *Map showing areas taken over by Israel in the Six Day War.*

Every cloud has a silver lining

'Out of the ashes of this disastrous war will arise the phoenix of a free Arab Palestine.'

(Yasser Arafat on the Six Day War. The phoenix was an imaginary bird that died in a fire and then rose from the ashes to fly again)

This disaster, though hard for all Arabs to swallow, offered a great opportunity to **Fatah**. It alone remained unbeaten, and the new flood of **refugees** created by the Israeli occupations promised many new recruits. Arafat and his **Palestinian** fighters were suddenly the one great hope of the Arab world.

Karameh and after

A few days after the war finished, Arafat slipped across the border and into the Israeli-occupied West Bank. He spent three months moving between hiding places, in a variety of disguises, making contacts and establishing **cells** of new recruits. It was too soon to challenge the Israeli occupation openly, but his presence offered hope for the future.

Once back on the east bank of the River Jordan, Arafat set up more training camps for the rush of new volunteers, and raised funds. In 1964, the Egyptians had set up an organization called the **Palestine Liberation Organization (PLO)**, which Fatah now joined. As the largest of the Palestinian fighting groups they insisted on a majority of the seats on the PLO's National Council, and Arafat became the leader of the organization in all but name.

▲ *Arafat in an underground command post, one of his hiding places during military operations.*

The raids across the Jordan River went on and provoked increasingly violent responses from the Israelis. In March 1968, the Israeli Army attacked the village of Karameh where Arafat had his headquarters. Other Palestinian groups withdrew but Arafat fought back. The Israeli attack, when it came, was finally repelled by Jordanian Army tank fire, but Arafat and his Fatah fighters had fought with skill and courage.

Across the Arab world Karameh was celebrated as a glorious victory, and Arafat became an overnight hero. His picture popped up everywhere, from back street Arab bars to the cover of *Time* magazine. Suddenly the whole world seemed aware of him and the Palestinian cause. Funds and recruits poured into PLO offices.

Arafat, not for the last time, managed to turn a victory into a partial defeat. His unwillingness to **delegate authority** and his inability to organize properly meant that the new volunteers were not turned into an efficient fighting force. His refusal to keep proper financial records meant that much of the money flooding into the PLO was either wasted on unnecessary things or disappeared into officials' pockets. But after Karameh, he was virtually irreplaceable as the number one symbol of Palestinian resistance.

▶ *Arafat, recently elected leader of the PLO, sits in Cairo's Koubbeh Republican Palace with Egyptian President Nasser, 11 March 1969.*

The PLO

The PLO or Palestine Liberation Organization was set up in 1964 to unite the many different Palestinian groups who wished to oppose Israeli occupation of Arab Palestine. By 1968 it was dominated by Arafat's Fatah, but there were 30 or so other member groups, some of which, like the pro-terrorist Popular Front for the Liberation of Palestine (PFLP), were highly influential. The Palestinian National Council (PNC) was set up to act as the PLO's parliament, and a Palestinian National Charter was created to set out the organization's policy and goals.

In early 1969 Arafat became Chairman of the PLO, and it would have to live with both his good qualities and his bad.

Thrown out of Jordan

By this time it was clear to most Palestinian fighters that it was going to take more than a few cross-border raids to make an impression on Israel. Some decided that a more peaceful approach was needed, but they received little encouragement from either Israel or their fellow Palestinians. Others decided that a tougher, more violent policy was called for, and over the next few years several groups within the PLO carried out a succession of plane **hijackings** and other **terrorist** attacks.

Arafat and most of the Fatah leadership probably opposed this wave of terrorism. Although it kept the Palestinian cause in the headlines, it also allowed enemies to brand all Palestinians as terrorists. But despite their disapproval, Arafat and the other Fatah leaders were reluctant to condemn or even discipline the hijackers. They were too frightened of splitting and weakening the PLO.

▲ Arab heads of state (Libyan leader Muammar Khadafy, Arafat, Egyptian President Nasser and King Hussein of Jordan) meet to put an end to the civil war between the Palestinians and the Jordanian government. The talks were unsuccessful.

In the meantime, the Palestinian fighters' behaviour in Jordan was putting the whole organization at risk. After Karameh they began behaving as if they were above the law, demanding payments, putting up road-blocks and engaging in various criminal activities. In September 1970 the country's ruler, King Hussein, finally lost patience with his ill-behaved guests. He turned his army loose, and after weeks of bitter and bloody fighting the Palestinian fighters were defeated. In 1971 they were forced out of Jordan altogether. Arafat had failed to control his own troops and he had underestimated King Hussein. Fatah was forced to set up a new home in Lebanon.

Black years

The PLO now found it more difficult to mount operations against Israel, and terrorism seemed, to many, the only way to keep the Palestinian cause alive. A new group called Black September (after the month of Hussein's attack) came into being, its members drawn mostly from Fatah.

Over the next two years it mounted a series of terrorist attacks, the most infamous of which involved the murder of eleven Israeli athletes at the Munich Olympics of 1972. Arafat may or may not have supported these attacks, but he knew that condemning them would leave him isolated and might well cost him his leadership of the PLO. He waited until it was clear the attacks were doing more harm than good to the PLO before stepping in to stop them.

Not that he had any real alternative to offer. In early 1973 he had few options open to him. Neither the armed struggle to reclaim Palestine nor terrorism had worked, so there was only **diplomacy** left. The Israelis would not talk to him, however, and his own people would not let him talk to the Israelis.

There was some good news: Hussein's brutality in 1970–71 made it unlikely that the Palestinian population of the West Bank would ever wish to be reunited with Jordan, and the Israeli seizure of land, theft of water resources and building of **settlements** made it certain their occupation would never be accepted. The Palestinians in the **occupied territories** still wanted to be ruled by the PLO, but how was Arafat to get the Israelis out?

That same year he also suffered a personal loss. In 1971, he had fallen in love with Nada Yashrouti, a PLO organizer in Lebanon. According to Arafat she had agreed to marry him, but in 1973 she was murdered in Beirut by an unknown gunman.

Lebanon

In autumn 1973 Egypt and Syria, driven to desperation by Israel's refusal to return the territories occupied in 1967, launched the October – or Yom Kippur – War. Despite early **Arab** successes, it was another overwhelming victory for Israel. At first it seemed like nothing had changed, but in fact the consequences of this war were far-reaching. The USA and the Soviet Union had been brought to the brink of a **nuclear confrontation** by their support for the opposing sides, and the oil-rich Arab states, angry at Western powers for supporting Israel, had temporarily refused to supply them with the oil their economies needed. It was becoming clear that a solution to the long Arab–Israeli conflict was not only desirable for those in the Middle East, it was in everyone's interests. In December 1973, all of the parties were called to a peace conference in Geneva.

The olive branch

The Geneva talks achieved little, but a process had been set in motion. Arafat, the **Palestinians** and all the other Arab states now had a clear choice to make. They could follow the old path of armed struggle and continue to hope for the dismantling of Israel, or they could take the new path of **diplomacy**, which involved accepting Israel's right to exist. For Arafat the choice was easy: diplomacy might or might not lead to an acceptable settlement for the Palestinians, but there was no future in armed struggle or **terrorism**.

At first, the new policy seemed to work well. An Arab summit in October 1974 agreed that the **PLO** was the only true representative of the Palestinian people. This meant that if the Israelis could be forced out of the **West Bank** and the **Gaza Strip**, then these territories would not be returned to Jordan and Egypt, but would form an independent Palestine.

A month later Arafat enjoyed an even greater triumph at the **United Nations (UN)**. His 80-minute speech ended with the lines: 'Today I have come bearing an olive branch [a traditional symbol of peace] and a freedom fighter's gun. Do not let the olive branch fall from my hand!' Both peace and war were possible, but he would prefer peace. Leaving the stage he clasped his hands above his head like a victorious boxer. It was a moment that Palestinians world-wide still remember, the moment when the rest of the world listened to their leader and their cause.

It was only a beginning. In 1977, the American President Carter declared his support for an undefined 'Palestinian homeland', but linked this with a Palestinian acceptance of UN Resolution 242 (see page 30), which, among other things, required an acceptance of Israel's right to exist. Arafat was tempted, but even Abu Jihad and Abu Iyad refused to support him in taking such a step. At the very least, they argued, the PLO needed a simultaneous recognition by Israel of the Palestinians' right to independence.

◀ *Arafat addresses the General Assembly of the United Nations on 12 November 1974.*

Resolution 242

UN Resolution 242, which was passed unanimously by the members of the UN Security Council in late 1967, asked for:

- the withdrawal of Israeli armed forces from **occupied territories**
- respect for the sovereignty, territorial integrity and political independence of every state in the area, and their right to live in peace within secure and recognized boundaries, free from threats or acts of force [every state in the area would be allowed to govern itself within borders that all its neighbours would respect]
- a just settlement of the **refugee** problem [there were large numbers of Palestinian refugees in all the Arab states bordering Israel]

President Carter succeeded in persuading Egypt's President Sadat and Israel's Prime Minister Begin to reach a peace agreement between their two countries at Camp David in 1978, but there was nothing in this agreement for the Palestinians. Indeed, many Arabs thought Sadat had betrayed the Palestinian cause by signing it.

His finest hour

By this time the Palestinian fighters were fully engaged in the Lebanese **civil war**, which had broken out in 1975–76, and which raged on into the early 1980s. In June 1982 the Israelis, tired of the instability on their northern border and seeking to either push out or destroy the PLO, launched an all-out invasion. It was the first real war between Israelis and Palestinians, with 75,000 Israeli troops facing roughly

15,000 Palestinian fighters under Arafat's command. The Palestinians received no help from the other Arab states, and the Americans, who alone could have restrained the Israelis, made no attempt to do so.

The Lebanese Civil War

Lebanon was already a deeply divided country when the Palestinian fighting groups arrived from Jordan. There was a long history of hostility between the country's **Christian** and **Muslim** communities, and the arrival of the Palestinians in 1971 was only one of several reasons for the outbreak of full-scale civil war in 1975. The Palestinians formed an alliance with the Lebanese Muslims, and the Christians were soon receiving help from Israel. Despite various interventions (by Syria, the rest of the Arab world, and Israel) the civil war dragged on for over a decade, with countless small areas ruled by local **militias**. The near-constant fighting between these militias caused many thousands of **civilian** casualties.

Muslim militiamen defend a position in Beirut during the Lebanese civil war.

As usual the two sides of Arafat were on display. His preparations had been disorganized and many Palestinian units were led by second-rate soldiers. Yet, once again, he inspired the ordinary Palestinian soldiers with his personal bravery and flair for the dramatic gesture. He was always amongst them, touring the front lines and putting himself at risk. He knew the Israelis were trying to kill him and the other PLO leaders, and his 'dog's sense' came in handy. These weeks in Lebanon were, as one journalist put it, 'his finest hour.'

There was no hope of victory, only of choosing the manner of defeat. Some PLO leaders wanted to fight to the death in a blaze of glory, but Arafat and the majority wanted to evacuate Beirut and concentrate on political activity in the occupied territories. In early August they negotiated a dignified withdrawal. Arafat himself was the last to leave, holding up a two-fingered 'victory' sign as his boat slipped away from the Lebanese coast.

Commander

'The worse it got, the more remarkable was his ability to rise to the occasion; it was as if he was made for battle. He slept in the backs of cars, operated from positions too near the Israeli forward lines to be believed, moved constantly, misled informers by arranging appointments at which he never showed up, and did anything else he could think of to avoid becoming a sitting target. Since he had no fixed headquarters safe from attack, many of his orders were issued while he was standing in the middle of streets or travelling in cars.'

(Said Aburish, describing Arafat's leadership during the battle for Beirut)

Sabra and Chatilla

The Israelis had promised that the Palestinian civilians left behind would be treated fairly, but in mid-September their troops deliberately allowed Lebanese Christian forces into the Palestinian **refugee camps** at Sabra and Chatilla in southern Beirut. Thousands of refugees were slaughtered. An outcry followed, and there was a worldwide wave of sympathy for the Palestinians and their cause. There were even huge demonstrations in Israel itself against the policy of the Israeli government, most of them sponsored by a new movement called 'Peace Now'. The PLO had been driven out of Lebanon, but a fair peace for the Palestinians was beginning to seem possible.

▲ Palestinian women search through the dead for their loved ones after the massacre at the Sabra refugee camp, September 1983.

Exile in Tunis

The **Palestinian** fighting groups forced to leave Lebanon in 1982 were scattered among several **Arab** states. Arafat and the **PLO** leadership established their new headquarters in the North African country of Tunisia. In both Jordan and Lebanon they had been within touching distance of the land they still called home, but now they were separated by 2200 kilometres (1400 miles) of Mediterranean Sea.

Arafat first, PLO second

Arafat's first task was to secure his own position as leader. His leadership in the Lebanon had impressed the world and ordinary Palestinians, but not his colleagues in the PLO. They criticized his dictatorial ways and his habit of preferring loyal helpers to efficient ones. Many still opposed his decision to abandon the armed struggle and were afraid of how much he might give away in negotiations with the Israelis.

Arafat argued and charmed and frequently threatened to resign. He appointed more friends to influential positions and reorganized things so that people reported only to him. Money was power, and he made sure that all the PLO's income was under his personal control. These changes made the PLO more inefficient, but they also made it harder for anyone to dislodge Arafat as its leader.

Many of Arafat's colleagues disliked his new willingness to work with their old enemy King Hussein of Jordan. But Arafat knew that the Israelis and Americans, both of whom still refused to recognize the PLO, would only allow him to participate in a peace conference as part of a Jordanian team. He needed King Hussein's help to get him through the conference room door.

Home routine

Arafat lived in a modest house in the Hamman Al Shat district of Tunis. His days usually began around 10 a.m. with a ride on his exercise bike. He refused to shave, claiming that the effort would cost him seven and a half hours each month. This, he said, was 'too much, because I have no time as it is'. For breakfast he had cornflakes with honey and tea, for lunch fish and yoghurt. He loved fruit, and was fond of snacking on honey and halvah (a crumbly sweet made from sesame flour and honey) late at night. He never drank coffee or alcohol, never smoked.

▲ *Tunis, the capital of Tunisia in North Africa, where Arafat lived in exile after the PLO defeat in Lebanon in 1982.*

Between meals Arafat's life was filled with attending meetings, phone calls, sending and answering faxes. He spoke to Arab leaders, to PLO people around the world, to journalists, to anyone he thought might be useful.

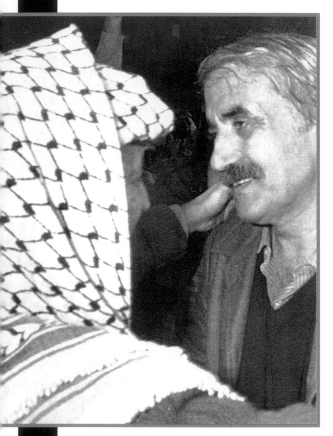

▲ *Arafat embraces George Habash, leader of the PFLP, after a meeting of the Palestine National Council in Algiers, February 1983.*

Now in his fifties, Arafat took care of his health. He took vitamins, had regular check-ups and forced himself to take a half-hour walk each afternoon. A trusted assistant prepared all his food, in case any of his many enemies were thinking of trying to poison him.

As it happened, the most serious threat to his life during this period came from the sky. On 1 October 1985, Israeli planes attacked Tunis, targeting PLO headquarters and Arafat's house. The raid, which Israel claimed was in retaliation for a PLO attack a week earlier, killed 58 Palestinians and 14 Tunisians, and reduced Arafat's house to rubble, but Arafat himself escaped unharmed. He claimed he was out jogging at the time.

Losing ground

The sense of relief did not last long. A week later one of the smaller groups attached to the PLO **hijacked** the *Achille Lauro* cruise liner in the Mediterranean and murdered one of the passengers. Arafat's refusal to condemn the hijacking – he was reluctant to lose the support of the hijackers' leader – enraged both the Egyptians and Americans.

Two months later Arafat fell out with King Hussein once more. The King had finally tired of waiting for Arafat to accept Resolution 242 (see page 30). In both cases, Arafat refused to say what the West wanted to hear because he knew that his own people would not accept it. Retaining his position as Chairman of the PLO was more important to him than pleasing the international community.

Holding court

'In meetings with rich Palestinians and others, Arafat's Tunis office was run like the diwan [court] of an Arab king. As in the past, even his most important meetings were interrupted by a flow of people who carried small pieces of paper and whispered in his ear to seek approval for whatever they were requesting. At night he would gather between ten and twenty people around him – being invited to dinner with him was a more accurate measure of one's importance than title or position.'

(Arafat biographer Said Aburish)

In Tunis the dinners and arguments went on into the small hours, but to outsiders it seemed as if the PLO were slowly sinking. Money poured out of the PLO bank accounts, often to be wasted on luxuries like private jet flights, but the amount pouring in grew less and less as the organization's popularity among the Arab states declined. By early 1987, Arafat and the PLO looked like a penniless king and his penniless court trapped in permanent **exile**.

Intifada

On 8 December 1987, four **Palestinian** youths were killed in a road accident in the **Gaza Strip**. There were rumours that the youths had been deliberately run down by an Israeli, and at the funeral an angry young Palestinian threw a stone at the watching Israeli soldiers. He was shot dead.

As the news spread, riots erupted throughout the Gaza Strip, and in the weeks that followed uproar spread through the **West Bank**. Streets were barricaded with heaps of burning tyres; thousands of children, women and old men threw stones at the Israeli security forces. The people of the **occupied territories**, tired of waiting for the now distant **PLO** or the other **Arab** states to liberate them, were taking matters into their own hands. An *intifada*, or uprising, had begun.

Taken by surprise, the Israelis reacted harshly. Soldiers, given the choice of retreating or opening fire, often opened fire. However, each dead Palestinian youth only brought forth a new hail of stones, and as the weeks went by world opinion turned against Israel. These were not **terrorists** or armed raiders, they were children, and television audiences around the world saw them beaten or killed just for demanding their freedom.

Arafat and the *intifada*

Arafat's first reaction was surprise, his second, anxiety. The uprising could collapse, and he was reluctant to support something that might fail and make the PLO look weak. On the other hand, the uprising might get bigger and make the PLO look irrelevant, which would be even more of a disaster. For several weeks he watched and waited, until he was sure that the uprising was not going to go away. He then took steps to bring it under PLO control. Abu Jihad was put in charge of organizing support for the protesters, of channelling money, for example, to those families who had members in jail.

▲ *Israeli soldiers open fire on stone-throwing children in the Gaza Strip during the first* intifada.

The neighbouring Arab states were also torn two ways. They welcomed the uprising at first, but soon became worried that similar displays of popular discontent might spread to their own countries. They gave the PLO more money to run the *intifada*, and to keep it within bounds.

Through 1988 the uprising showed no signs of weakening, and Arafat continued to worry that it might affect his own authority. **Islamic fundamentalist** groups like Islamic Jihad and Hamas were growing stronger and posing the first real threat to the PLO's hold over the occupied territories. The increasing popularity of local PLO leaders like Hanan Ashrawi and Faisal Husseini also posed a potential threat to Arafat's position. He may even have had doubts about giving Abu Jihad the important job of organizing the *intifada*, but if so the doubts had no time to grow. In April 1988, an Israeli hit squad murdered Arafat's old friend in his Tunisian home.

One step forward, one step back

The *intifada* went on. Arafat knew there was no way stone-throwing children could physically force the Israelis out of the occupied territories, but he hoped world opinion would shame them into withdrawing, or at least into being more flexible than they would otherwise have been. He decided that the PLO could further encourage Israel by demonstrating its own flexibility.

In November 1988, the **Palestine National Council (PNC)** finally accepted Resolution 242, which, among other things, guaranteed Israel's right to exist. In return, the PNC demanded the creation of a Palestinian state in the occupied territories of the West Bank and Gaza Strip. Arafat repeated this message to the **United Nations** the following month, and added that the PLO had now completely abandoned terrorism. This was what the Americans had long waited to hear, and 20 years after Karameh, Washington finally agreed to talk to the PLO.

◀ *Abu Jihad, one of Arafat's oldest and most trusted lieutenants, who was assassinated by the Israelis in April 1988.*

Intifada incident

'The soldiers caught a child. The commander arrived, he grabbed the child and told him: "Climb up on the electrical pole" – it was a high-tension wire – "and take down the PLO flag."

'It was a huge pole, impossible to climb. He started and after a few metres he could not go on. The commander started to hit the child in the legs and told him to go on climbing. I was in shock but the soldiers were enjoying it.

'... I started crying. I started to fight with the commander. He said: "They put it there. They can take it down." I asked: "How will they get it down? It's impossible." We were actually fighting in front of the soldiers, and finally he gave in. They did not bring down the flag.'

(An Israeli named Alon, describing an incident of the *intifada* which took place during his military service on the West Bank)

Arafat thought he had made a breakthrough, but the Israelis refused to believe the PLO's promises or weaken their grip on the occupied territories. The Americans listened to the PLO, but put no real pressure on the Israelis. The *intifada* went on through 1989 and 1990, its impact on world opinion slowly fading, and in the occupied territories the apparent failure of Arafat's **diplomacy** saw increasing support for the Islamic fundamentalist groups. When the Soviet Union collapsed, many Russian **Jews emigrated** to Israel and settled on the West Bank, the very land Arafat hoped would form his state of Palestine. Despite all the advances the PLO had made over the years, the situation in 1990 seemed to be getting worse rather than better.

▲ *Palestinians waving Palestinian flags during a protest march in Gaza.*

In desperation Arafat turned to the man many saw as the Arab world's rising power – Iraq's Saddam Hussein. The long Iran–Iraq war had recently ended in a bloody tie, but the ambitious Saddam had retained his huge army. Here, Arafat thought, was a possible counterweight to the power of Israel.

Desperate measures

When Saddam Hussein invaded Kuwait in August 1990, Arafat refused to condemn him. Faced with demands from both Western and Arab states to withdraw, Saddam offered to leave Kuwait if the Israelis left the **occupied territories**, and Arafat offered his full support. Many of his colleagues in the **PLO** disagreed with him – they argued that Saddam's occupation of Kuwait weakened their case against the Israeli occupation – but Arafat had most ordinary Palestinians on his side. They considered Saddam a hero for standing up to Israel and the West.

▶ *Arafat is welcomed in Baghdad by Iraqi leader Saddam Hussein on 27 August 1990, three weeks after the Iraqi invasion of Kuwait.*

The Western powers and their Arab allies were determined that Saddam should not profit from his **aggression**, and over the next few months a huge military force was assembled in northern Saudi Arabia. 1991 opened very badly for Arafat. His old companion Abu Iyad, who had opposed Saddam's occupation of Kuwait, was killed by pro-Iraqi **Palestinians**, and then Saddam's army was ejected from Kuwait by the Americans and their allies. Arafat had supported the wrong side.

Kuwait, Saudi Arabia and the United Arab Emirates, all furious with Arafat for supporting Saddam, cut off their financial support for the PLO, bringing the organization close to financial ruin once more.

The Madrid Conference

Not all was lost. While Saddam was still in Kuwait, the Western powers refused to admit any similarity between his occupation and the Israeli occupation of the **West Bank** and the **Gaza Strip**, but once he had been ejected, America's Arab allies made it clear that they expected some progress in the other, much longer-running dispute.

Illegal settlements?

'The occupying power shall not deport or transfer parts of its own civilian population into the territory it occupies'.

(Article 49 of the **Geneva Convention** relative to the Protection of **Civilian** Persons in Times of War, which came into force in October 1950. This is the international law which Palestinians claim Israel has broken with its building of **settlements** in the occupied territories.)

Towards the end of 1991, a conference was called in Madrid. Israel was pressured into attending by America, who held back loans. The Palestinians agreed to be included as part of the Jordanian team when the Americans promised no more Israeli settlements and the handing over of at least a part of the occupied territories to Palestinian control. The Israelis still refused to talk directly to any member of the PLO, so Arafat ran things from faraway Tunis, often bringing the entire negotiating team by plane from Madrid to instruct them on a particular issue.

American promises were one thing; getting the Israelis to fulfil them was more difficult. The Madrid conference gave way to two-sided negotiations in Washington, but through the opening months of 1992 there were no obvious signs of progress.

A brush with death

In April 1992, Arafat was flying back to Tunis above the Libyan desert when his small plane, delayed by strong winds, ran out of fuel and crashed. For thirteen hours no one knew whether he was dead or alive. An American satellite eventually located the wreckage, and thirteen hours after the crash a rescue team reached the shattered aircraft. The pilot and two other passengers were dead but Arafat was only injured. In hospital a blood clot was removed from his brain, and soon he was enjoying reading the summaries of his life achievements that had appeared in the newspapers. The fact that the occupied territories had come to a virtual standstill while people waited for news of his fate pleased him immensely.

Soon after this, the news leaked out that he had been married for two years to Suha, the daughter of well-known Palestinian **Christian** politician Raymonda Tawil. Suha was 34 years younger than the 63-year-old Arafat. The two had met in Jordan in 1985, and again in 1988 when Suha began work as a messenger between the West Bank and Tunis. Arafat eventually admitted he was married, but refused to say anything else. Like most of his countrymen, he disapproved of discussing family matters in public.

▶ *Suha Arafat walks down the steps of the family home in Gaza.*

The Oslo Agreement

The talks in Washington made little progress, but late in 1992 a chance meeting between Norwegian and Israeli **academics** led to a series of secret, semi-official talks between Palestinian and Israeli teams in Oslo. Free from the pressures of media interest, the talks went better than anyone had hoped, and in August a surprised world heard that an agreement had been reached. In exchange for Palestinian recognition of Israel, the Israelis offered (a) recognition of the PLO as the sole representatives of the Palestinian people and (b) the granting of limited **autonomy** – responsibility for health, sanitation, education and postal services – in the Gaza Strip and the West Bank town of Jericho.

Many Palestinians were more struck by what the agreement left out. There was no mention of land rights or water resources, of Palestinian **refugees** or Israeli settlements. There was no mention of Jerusalem or a Palestinian state. Although all these issues were down for discussion in three years' time, the PLO seemed to have granted a big favour – the recognition of Israel – in return for very little. When attacked by his colleagues for agreeing to such a deal, Arafat told them that the PLO's near-bankruptcy (financial ruin) had left him no choice.

The showman

Only hours before the September signing ceremony was due to take place in Washington, Arafat told the Americans that he wanted to bring his gun with him. When the Americans refused to allow this, Arafat suggested that he could dramatically let the gun drop to the floor as a sign of his commitment to peace. It was only when this too was refused that he reluctantly agreed to leave the gun behind.

On 13 September 1993, Arafat and Israeli Prime Minister
Itzhak Rabin signed the agreement in Washington. America's
President Clinton then nudged the two men towards shaking
hands. A beaming Arafat immediately extended his, but a TV
audience of millions watched Rabin struggle to overcome his
reluctance to do likewise. Their hands did meet, but in that
moment of hesitation real peace still seemed a long way off.

▲ *Encouraged by US President Clinton, Israeli Premier Yitzhak Rabin
reluctantly shakes hands with Arafat on the White House lawn,
13 September 1993.*

Homeland

Arafat shrugged aside criticism of his agreement with Israel, calling the critics 'enemies of peace'. He had given up more than many **Palestinians** wanted, but there were many others who believed he had achieved all that was possible, at least for the moment. In May 1994 the handover of power in the **Gaza Strip** and Jericho began, and in July Arafat returned to assume the leadership of the new **Palestine National Authority** (**PNA**). He had not set foot on Palestinian soil for 27 years, and hundreds of thousands turned out to greet him. Whatever their doubts about the agreement, the Palestinians had recovered a small part of their homeland, and they celebrated that fact.

Arafat enjoyed the moment, but his continuing negotiations with Israel were already in difficulty. **Extremists** on each side refused to accept a compromise settlement, and moderates on each side lacked the power to impose one. Arafat, Rabin and Rabin's Foreign Minister Shimon Peres were awarded the Nobel Peace Prize that autumn, but the growing death toll from **terrorist** bombings and Israeli **reprisals** emphasized the lack of a real peace.

▶ *Arafat is carried in triumph into the new Palestinian homeland, July 1994.*

In November 1995, an Israeli extremist assassinated Prime Minister Rabin, and six months later his successor, Shimon Peres, was defeated in a general election by the more aggressive Binyamin Netanyahu. The slow-moving negotiations between Israel and the Palestinians ground to a halt.

▲ West Bank PLO leader Hanan Ashrawi and Arafat meet ex-President George Bush, George W. Bush's father, in Washington DC.

No democracy

The political situation inside the PNA was just as worrying. There had been no elections in 1994 – the **PLO** had simply arrived from Tunis and taken over – and the elections held in 1996 seemed less than fair to many observers. Neither Arafat nor his colleagues were used to operating a democracy, and no real attempt was made to create one. All the old problems of **favouritism**, inefficiency and **corruption** were recreated in their new home.

In Tunis, the PLO had been responsible only for itself. In Gaza, the failure to establish an independent **judiciary**, or indeed a rule of law, soon led to serious **human rights** violations. Arafat and the Israelis were both keen to crack down on **Islamic fundamentalist** groups, and imprisonment without trial, torture, and deaths in custody soon became commonplace. Newspapers that protested were closed down.

Wife and daughter

Arafat took up residence on the ground floor of an old British Governor's residence in Gaza, but the two rooms were hardly enough for him, Suha, and his security men. After Suha gave birth to their daughter Zahwa – named after Arafat's mother – in the summer of 1995, she insisted they take over the second floor as well. Arafat reportedly looked at the newly decorated rooms, told her it looked like a **cabaret**, and went back downstairs.

◀ *Arafat's wife Suha and daughter Zahwa.*

Over the next few years, Suha became popular in her own right. She did a lot of work for charity organizations in the PNA, concentrating on women's and children's issues, and was not afraid to criticize her husband's government. On one occasion she said that she had *'married a myth'*, but that the marriage had 'helped him step down from his pedestal and become a human being'. He still spent too much time at work, but his daughter, according to Suha, had 'softened' him. Zahwa was said to enjoy sitting on her daddy's knee and pointing out the famous leaders on television news broadcasts.

A second *intifada*

In autumn 1998, US President Clinton tried to get the 'peace process' started once more. At a meeting in Maryland the Israelis agreed to hand over another 13 per cent of the **occupied territories**, but when the five-year limit set by the Oslo Agreement expired in May 1999 most of the key issues were still in dispute. A victory for the peace-minded Ehud Barak in the Israeli election a few weeks later offered hope, and later that year Arafat and Barak signed another **provisional agreement**: the Palestinians would be granted self-rule in the West Bank by September 2000, provided that other outstanding issues could be agreed.

They could not. The negotiators could not agree on a final border between the two countries or on what to do about the Israeli **settlements**, and Israel refused to consider any Palestinian return to the homes which had been lost in 1948. Barak's government was apparently prepared to make some concessions over Jerusalem, but fewer than the PLO demanded, and probably more than most Israelis were willing to accept. The September 2000 deadline came and went with no sign of a solution.

The people of the occupied territories took to the streets in a second *intifada*; the people of Israel responded by electing Ariel Sharon as their Prime Minister. Sharon's record, which included military triumphs in most of Israel's wars, also included responsibility for an infamous killing spree in one Palestinian village, Qibwa, almost 50 years earlier. In 1983 he had been forced to resign as Defence Minister in the aftermath of the massacres at Sabra and Chatilla. He was not a very likely partner for peace.

The new *intifada* continued into 2001. By May, over 500 had died, 90 percent of them Palestinians. Israeli reprisals for terrorist attacks grew more extreme, and several of Arafat's aides were targeted. It is not known whether there were attempts to kill Arafat himself, but, as so often in the past, he was probably moving his office from house to house, trying to keep one step ahead of his enemies. He might have been the President of the PNA, but he was still a long way from being the President of a truly independent Palestinian state at peace with its Israeli neighbour.

Ask anyone in the world to name a single **Palestinian**, and the chances are that they will name Yasser Arafat. He has played a prominent role in his nation's affairs since his student days more than a half a century ago, and over the last three decades his name has become completely identified with the struggle to establish a Palestinian state.

Key decisions

On three occasions Arafat made decisions which were to prove crucial for the Palestinian cause. During the war of 1948–49 and in the years of *fedayeen* raids that followed, he became convinced that the other **Arab** states would never win back Palestine for the Palestinians, and that the Palestinians, as a consequence, would have to do it for themselves. Arafat, Abu Iyad and Abu Jihad formed **Fatah** with this in mind. Fatah would accept help from anyone, but would rely on no one.

▲ *An Israeli soldier about to throw a stun grenade at Palestinian medics during clashes in the West Bank town of Ramallah, March 2001.*

After the Six Day War had proved once again that the Arab states were no match for Israel, Arafat and Fatah took the decision to launch a sustained armed struggle in the newly **occupied territories** of the **West Bank** and **Gaza Strip**. The Battle of Karameh in March 1968 was not a military victory in any real sense, but it turned Arafat into a hero. In retrospect, it summed up the whole armed struggle – the military impact was minimal but the political and emotional value was immense. The armed struggle brought the Palestinian cause to world attention, and it kept the hopes of ordinary Palestinians alive.

After the 1973 war, Arafat was the first to realize that something new was needed. In the long run Israel could not be destroyed, and Arafat knew it. His third key decision was to abandon the armed struggle and opt for **diplomacy**, to try and talk his way to a solution which both sides could accept. With opinions so divided among the Palestinians, it has proved an incredibly difficult job. At times his own failures – to organize, to oppose **corruption**, to choose independently minded colleagues – have made it seem almost impossible.

Over the years he succeeded in lowering the expectations of most Palestinians to a more realistic level. The notion of destroying Israel, of taking back *all* the land that the Palestinians felt had been stolen from them in 1948–49 and 1967, was slowly cast aside. In its place Arafat offered a two-state solution: the Palestinians would accept Israel in return for their own state in those territories occupied since 1967. Progress towards this goal, though slow and fitful, has been made, and in 1994 Arafat could at last assume limited control over a small portion of Palestinian territory. In the following years the two sides moved closer to a lasting agreement without actually achieving one. By late 2000 the so-called 'peace process' was once more at a virtual standstill.

Into the 21st century

The situation confronting Arafat in May 2001 was in many
ways as difficult as any that he had faced during the years of
exile. There were too many people to keep happy, too many
balls for Arafat the political juggler to keep in the air. While
the Israelis demanded more concessions, the **Islamic
fundamentalists** demanded fewer; he could not satisfy the
one without risking a violent reaction from the other. He
needed the economic aid which the USA and the richer Arab
states were providing, but they too were pressuring him to
give up more than most Palestinians were prepared to accept.
The better-educated among his people were also demanding a
democratic political system, yet his natural inclination, his
experience in exile and the security needs of the current
situation, were all encouraging him to become more

dictatorial. At this
point in time the
presidency of the
**Palestinian National
Authority** would have
tested any politician,
and it would be harsh
to condemn Arafat for
his failure to rise above
such difficulties.

◀ *Telling it like it is: Arafat at
a press conference in Paris,
May 2001.*

It is hard to imagine that anyone else could have brought the Palestinian cause further towards its goal of independence than Arafat, and if an independent Palestinian state is finally established then he will rightly be honoured as its father. If and when that time comes, the Palestinian people may do well to have someone else in charge of that state, to take on the responsibility of running a modern democratic society.

The real Arafat?

'In Tunisia in 1987 Arafat shocked and amused an Iraqi academic who politely suggested that many Arab leaders accused him, Arafat, of lying .... Staring at the Iraqi with incredulous [unbelieving], extra-bulging eyes, Arafat said, "Why not? For Palestine, I'd lie all the time." Momentarily, his guest was at a loss for words. Then he burst out laughing and Arafat joined him with a broad smile which, according to the Iraqi, lightened his face and made him look like a little boy.'

(An incident described by Said Aburish in his biography *Arafat: From Defender to Dictator*)

Timeline

1929	Yasser Arafat born August 24, probably in Cairo.
1933	Sent to relations in Jerusalem after mother's death.
1937	Returns from Jerusalem.
1939	World War II breaks out.
1947	**United Nations** (**UN**) votes to **partition** Palestine.
	Civil war in Palestine between **Jews** and **Arabs**.
1948	Establishment of the state of Israel.
	Arafat takes part in the fighting around Gaza.
1949–56	Student at University of Cairo.
1952	Free Officers Movement overthrows Egyptian monarchy.
1954–55	Arafat takes part in *fedayeen* raids into Israel from **Gaza Strip**.
1956	Attends student conference in Prague.
	Suez crisis and Israeli occupation of Sinai.
1957	Arafat takes job as engineer in Kuwait.
1959	Founds **Fatah** in Kuwait.
1961	Fatah begins recruiting fighters for the armed struggle.
1963	Arafat gives up job in Kuwait and moves to Syria.
1964	**PLO** founded in Egypt.
1965	First Fatah raids into Israel.
1967	Israel, victorious in Six Day (or June) War, occupies **West Bank**/Gaza Strip.
	Arafat personally infiltrates occupied West Bank.
1968	(21 March) Battle of Karameh.
	First **PFLP** hijacking.
1969	Arafat elected Chairman of PLO.
	Opposes **hijackings**.
1970–71	PLO expelled from Jordan, moves to Lebanon.
1972	Killing of Israeli athletes by Black September **terrorists** at Munich Olympics.
1973	Israel wins October (or Yom Kippur) War after initial Arab successes.

1974	Arafat addresses **United Nations** ('olive branch' – speech).
1975–76	Lebanon descends into civil war.
1982	(June) Israel invades Lebanon.
	(August) PLO forced out of Lebanon, moves HQ to Tunis.
	(September) Massacres at Sabra and Chatilla **refugee camps** in Beirut.
1983	Arafat faces serious opposition within the PLO.
1985	(October) Israeli attack on Tunis.
	(October) Hijacking of *Achille Lauro*.
1987	(December) *Intifada* begins in **occupied territories**.
1988	(April) Abu Jihad murdered by Israeli commandos in Tunis.
	(November) PLO recognizes Israel and renounces terrorism.
	(December) Arafat addresses UN in Geneva.
1989	Marries Suha Tawil.
1990	(August) Iraq invades Kuwait.
1991	(January) Abu Iyad murdered by pro-Iraqi **Palestinians**.
	(February) Gulf War between Iraq and US-led coalition.
	(October) Madrid Conference opens.
1992	(April) Arafat involved in desert plane crash.
1993	(September) Oslo Agreement, end of *intifada*.
1994	(July) Arafat returns to Palestine as leader of **Palestinian National Authority**.
	Awarded Nobel Peace Prize.
1995	(July) Birth of daughter Zahwa.
1996	(January) Arafat wins presidency of Palestinian National Authority with 88% of votes.
2000	(September) Second intifada begins.

Key people of Arafat's time

Abu Iyad (real name *Salah Khalaf*) (1933–91). A long-term colleague of Arafat and a founding member of **Fatah**. Chiefly responsible for security and intelligence within the **PLO**, he was assassinated by pro-Iraqi Palestinians.

Abu Jihad (real name *Khalil Al Wazir*) (1935–88). A long-term colleague of Arafat and a founding member of Fatah. Chiefly responsible for political organization within the PLO, he was assassinated by an Israeli hit squad in Tunis.

Ehud Barak (1942–). Israeli general and Prime Minister (1999–2001) who came close to reaching agreement with Arafat in 2000.

King Hussein of Jordan (1935–99) succeeded his father King Abdullah in 1953. He forced the Palestinian fighting groups out of Jordan in 1970–71, but eventually accepted that the **West Bank**, which Jordan had ruled between 1948 and 1967, should become part of an independent Palestine.

Saddam Hussein (1937–). President of Iraq since 1979. His army invaded neighbouring Kuwait in August 1990 but was ejected by a Western, American-led coalition in the 1991 Gulf War.

Mufti of Jerusalem (*Hajj Amin Al Husseini*)(1895–1974) led **Arab** resistance to the British policy of allowing massive **Jewish immigration** into Palestine between the two world wars.

Gamal Abdel Nasser (1918–70) led the Free Officers Movement which overthrew the Egyptian monarchy in 1952. Became President of Egypt in 1954. His defiance of the Western powers during the Suez Crisis made him a hero throughout the Arab world, but then his failures in the conflict with Israel weakened his reputation.

Binyamin Netanyahu (1949–). Israeli Prime Minister (1996–99) who slowed the peace process begun by Rabin and Peres.

Shimon Peres (1923–). Israeli politician, Prime Minister (1984–86 and 1995–96) and several times Foreign Minister, who is considered more peace-inclined than most of his colleagues.

Yitzhak Rabin (1922–95). Israeli soldier and Prime Minister (1974–77 and 1992–95). He took a hard line against the **intifada** but signed the Oslo Agreement with Arafat. In 1995 he was assassinated by an Israeli opposed to the peace process.

Ariel Sharon (1928–). Israeli general and politician, Prime Minister (2000–) known for his hostile attitude towards the Palestinians, and remembered by them for his alleged involvement in the massacres at Qibwa (1953) and Sabra/Chatilla (1982).

Further reading

Books

Arab–Israeli Conflict (Troubled World series), Ivan Minnis, Heinemann Library, 2001

Conflict in Palestine, Josh Brooman, Longman, 1999

War and Peace in the Middle East (20th Century History series), Michael Scott-Baumann, Hodder, 1998

Sources

Arafat in the Eye of the Beholder, John and Janet Wallach, Lyle Stuart, 1990

Arafat: From Defender to Dictator, Said K. Aburish, Bloomsbury, 1998

The Fifty Years War, Ahron Bregman and Jihan El-Tahri, Penguin/BBC, 1998

Website

Arab culture site:
   http://arabculture.about.com/culture/arabculture/cs/yassirarafat

Glossary

academics university teachers

aggression unprovoked attack

Arab nationalism idea that Arab interests can best be promoted through **Arab unity**, and perhaps even the creation of a single Arab state

Arabs people who originated in present-day Arabia and who now form by far the largest group in most countries of the Middle East and North Africa. Most, but not all, Arabs are Muslims and most speak Arabic.

autonomy some degree of self-government, but not full independence

Balfour Declaration statement of support for the establishment of a Jewish national home in Palestine made by the British Foreign Secretary Arthur Balfour in November 1917

cabaret place of entertainment, often extravagantly decorated

cells in politics, small groups of activists

Christians believers in Christianity, one of the world's three major monotheistic (one God) religions (along with Islam and Judaism)

civilian person who is not a member of the armed forces

civil war war between different groups in one country

Communism political theory and practice which puts the interests of the society as a whole above the interest of individuals

corruption immoral practices like bribery and fraud

delegate authority when someone in power allows others to take at least some decisions for themselves

diaspora the dispersion or scattering of a people. Originally referred to the scattering of the Jewish people, but in recent times it has been used to describe the dispersion of other races like the Armenians and Palestinians.

diplomacy the management of relations between states by peaceful means

emigration leaving a country

exile someone who lives outside his or her own country, by choice or not

extremists people who hold extreme views, and who are usually unwilling to make compromises

(Al) Fatah political and military organization founded by Arafat and others in 1959, which later became the most powerful group within the Palestine Liberation Organization

favouritism the unfair favouring of one person or group rather than another

fedayeen Arab guerrilla fighters. In Arabic, *fedayeen* means 'self-sacrificer'

financial accountability keeping an honest record of money received and spent

Gaza Strip strip of land along the east Mediterranean coast, incorporating town of Gaza. Ruled by Britain 1918–48, Egypt 1948–67, Israel 1967–94, Palestinian National Authority 1994–present)

guerrilla fighters unofficial soldiers, who usually have to rely on surprise and movement in their campaigns against official forces

hijacking violent take-over, usually of a plane, ship or other means of transport

(the) Holocaust name given to the murder of six million Jews (half the Jewish population of Europe) by Nazi Germany during World War II

immigration coming in to a country

infiltration entry, often with the intention of remaining unnoticed

intifada Arabic word for 'uprising', the campaign of resistance to Israeli occupation of the West Bank and Gaza Strip which began in late 1987, ended in 1993 with the signing of the Oslo Agreement, and started up again in autumn 2000

Islam one of the three major monotheistic (one God) religions (along with Christianity and Judaism), founded by Prophet Muhammad in the 7th century

Islamic fundamentalist someone who believes in strictly following the rules – or a particular interpretation of the rules – of Islam's holy book, the *Koran*

Jews people descended from the ancient Israelites who, over the centuries, have been scattered around the world by persistent persecution. Six million European Jews were murdered in World War II by Nazi Germany and its allies. There are now approximately 18 million Jews worldwide, 40% of whom live in the USA, 20% in Israel.

judiciary those who run a country's legal system

militia non-professional unit of fighters

Mufti Islamic title for someone whose job covers political and religious duties

Muslim follower of Islam

Muslim Brotherhood Egyptian political group which wanted a more Islamic society

nationalist someone whose main political interest is in promoting the interests of his or her own nation

nationalize take into government ownership

nuclear confrontation international crisis in which one or more of the participants threatens to consider the use of nuclear weapons

occupied territories territories taken over and administered against the wishes of the inhabitants. In Arab–Israeli history, the phrase usually refers to the Palestinian territories occupied by Israel after its victory in the 1967 Six Day War: the Gaza Strip (which had been ruled by Egypt between 1949 and 1967) and the West Bank (which had been ruled by Jordan in the same period)

Palestine Liberation Organization (PLO) organization created in 1964 to bring together the many Palestinian political and military groups fighting for a Palestinian state

Palestinian National Authority (PNA) name given to the government of those areas of the occupied territories given limited self-rule in 1994

Palestinian National Charter document containing the policy and aims of the PLO

Palestine National Council (PNC) the parliament of the PLO

Palestinians originally those people who lived in Palestine (roughly defined as that area ruled by the British between 1918 and 1948). Since the creation of Israel in 1948, the Palestinian Jews have been known as Israelis, and the term Palestinian is now only used to describe the Palestinian Arabs.

persecute make life difficult for, ill-treat

Popular Front for the Liberation of Palestine (PFLP) Palestinian group belonging to the PLO which became infamous for hijackings and other terrorists activities

prisoners of conscience people imprisoned for their political or religious views

provisional agreement temporary agreement which will hopefully become permanent

public relations creation and development of favourable impressions and images

refugee camp place where refugees are housed, often in tents and usually on a temporary basis

refugees people who have been forced to leave their own countries

reprisals actions taken in retaliation for other actions

self-rule government by representatives of the people being governed

settlements in occupied territories, Israeli communities set up since 1967

Suez Canal Zone area of Egypt including the Suez Canal which the British continued to administer after the rest of Egypt had been given independence

terrorism use of violence and intimidation against ordinary people for political ends

United Nations (UN) international organization set up in 1945 to help settle disputes between nations, among other things

Western Wall wall in Jerusalem, sometimes known as the 'Wailing Wall', which forms part of buildings considered holy by Jews and Muslims

West Bank hilly area west of the Jordan river approximately 110 kilometres long and 50 kilometres wide. Ruled by Britain 1918–48, Jordan 1948–67, Israel 1967–present. Since 1994, there has been a significant transfer of power in the towns to the Palestinian National Authority

Index